Investing Made Simple

Investing in Index Funds
Explained in 100 Pages or Less

Why is there a light bulb on the cover?

In cartoons and comics, a light bulb is often used to signify a moment of clarity or sudden understanding—an "aha!" moment. My hope is that the books in the *"...in 100 pages or less"* series can help readers achieve clarity and understanding of topics that are often considered complex and confusing—hence the light bulb.

Investing Made Simple

Investing in Index Funds Explained in 100 Pages or Less

Mike Piper, CPA

A note on the data used:
Except when stated otherwise, bond returns are calculated using the "Intermediate-Term Government Bonds" data series (which tracks the return of 5-year Treasury bonds) from the *2017 Stocks, Bonds, Bills, and Inflation (SBBI) Yearbook*, published by Wiley. Stock market returns are calculated using the "Large-Cap Stocks" data series (which currently tracks the S&P 500) from the *2017 Stocks, Bonds, Bills, and Inflation (SBBI) Yearbook*.

Dedication

To you, the reader, for taking the initiative
to take charge of your finances.

Your Feedback is Appreciated!

As the author of this book, I'm very interested to hear your thoughts. If you find the book helpful, please let me know! Alternatively, if you have any suggestions of ways to make the book better, I'm eager to hear that, too.

Finally, if you're dissatisfied with your purchase for any reason, let me know, and I'll be happy to provide you with a refund of the current list price of the book (limited to one refund per household).

You can reach me at: mike@simplesubjects.com.

Best Regards,
Mike Piper, CPA

Table of Contents

**Part Two:
Constructing a Portfolio**

Part Three:
Stay out of Trouble

INTRODUCTION

Investing is *Not* Complicated.

Many people seem to think that investing is a complicated, highly technical topic. It's really not. Or at least, it doesn't have to be. In fact, I'm confident that the majority of what you need to know about investing can be explained in just 100 pages. No need for a big, thick textbook. No need for an advanced degree in finance.

Of course, there's an entire industry built upon convincing us that investing *is* complicated. But we'll get to that later.

For now, just know that investing is something you're capable of understanding on your own. And, if you've found investing to be confusing in the past, it's probably due (at least in part) to the fact that you've been bombarded with a bunch of conflicting information from parties who are each more concerned with getting you to consume their products and services than they are with providing you with unbiased advice.

For example, the discount brokerage firms would have you believe that the path to investment success is to pick stocks (and to trade them frequently). The mutual fund industry, on the other hand, would make the case that you're better off having a professional pick the stocks for you. Whom should you believe?

Is This the Right Book for You?

To be entirely up front: Given its short length, this book is not going to turn you into an investing guru. And it's *certainly* not going to provide you with any sort of way to get rich overnight. That's not its goal. Its goal is simply to provide you with enough information to either:

- Get started investing for your future, or
- If you've already begun to invest, to take a look at your current strategy to see whether it could use any changes.

My hope is that you'll supplement the information you gain from this book with either:

- The services of a trustworthy, well-informed financial advisor—in Chapter 12 we discuss some tips for finding such a person—or
- An ongoing program of self-education, should you decide to handle your investments on your own. (Several suggestions for further reading are provided in the appendix.)

With that out of the way, let's get started, shall we?

PART ONE

Investing Basics

CHAPTER ONE

The Building Blocks

Before we can have any meaningful discussion about investing, we need to define the most basic building blocks of an investment portfolio: stocks, bonds, and mutual funds. We'll talk more in later chapters about the advantages and disadvantages of each of these investments—as well as how to determine how much of your portfolio to allocate to each. For now, let's just make sure we're up to speed on definitions.

Stocks

A stock (sometimes referred to as an "equity") is a piece of ownership in a company. The value of a stock lies in the fact that companies (usually) earn profits. Those profits are either:

a) Distributed to the shareholders (in a payment known as a dividend), or
b) Reinvested to grow the company (thereby hopefully increasing the value of the company and, eventually, the share price).

Bonds

A bond is a loan made by an investor to a company, a government, or a governmental agency. The value of a bond lies in the fact that the borrower agrees to pay interest to the lender.

Mutual Funds

A mutual fund is simply a collection of stocks, bonds, or other investments that has been chosen by a professional investor (known as a fund manager). Most mutual funds are known as "actively managed" funds because their fund managers are actively searching for investments that they believe will earn above-average returns.

Index Funds

Some mutual funds, however, are not actively managed, but "passively managed." These funds—

known as index funds—are designed to simply mimic the performance of a given index.

What's an index? In the field of investing, indexes are indicators that represent the value of a particular group of investments. For example, the S&P 500 is an index that tracks the performance of 500 of the largest companies in the United States. Therefore, an S&P 500 index fund is a mutual fund that owns shares of each of the companies in the S&P 500 and which should closely mimic the performance of the S&P 500 index.

There are indexes that track just about everything you could imagine, and more indexes (and index funds) are being created every year. Fortunately, you only need to know about a handful of different index funds in order to create a diversified portfolio.

Chapter 1 Simple Summary

- Stocks represent shares of ownership in a company. Stock investors seek to make money (either through dividend payments or through increased value of the company's stock) when the company earns a profit.

- Bonds are loans made by investors to corporations, governments, or governmental agencies. Bond investors seek to make money through the receipt of interest payments made by the borrower.

- Mutual funds are portfolios of investments that have been selected by a professional fund manager. Most funds are "actively managed" and seek to earn above-average returns.

- Index funds are "passively managed" mutual funds, which seek only to match the performance of a given index.

CHAPTER TWO

IRAs, 401(k)s, and Other Investment Accounts

Despite a common misconception to the contrary, IRAs and 401(k)s are *not* investments. Rather, they are types of investment *accounts* (in which you can invest in stocks, bonds, mutual funds, and so on). The reason these accounts are so important is that they have significant tax advantages over regular, fully taxable accounts. In order to make a meaningful comparison, however, we first need to briefly cover how regular brokerage accounts are taxed.

Taxable Accounts

In a regular, taxable brokerage account:

1. Interest that you receive (from a bond, for instance) is taxed as ordinary income.[1]
2. Most dividend income is taxed at a maximum tax rate of 20%.
3. Capital gains (i.e., gains from selling an asset that has appreciated in value) are taxed at a maximum rate of 20% if you've held the asset for more than one year, and taxed at your ordinary income tax rate if you've held the asset for one year or less.

The Benefits of Traditional IRAs

Traditional IRAs are simply investment accounts with some additional benefits and restrictions tacked on. Specifically, when you contribute money to a traditional IRA, you usually get a tax deduction for the amount of the contribution.

Also, as long as the money remains in the account, it grows tax-free. However, when you do take money out of the account, the entire withdrawal is taxable as ordinary income (unless you've made traditional IRA contributions for which you did not qualify for a deduction due to the income limits described later in this chapter).

---

[1] For reference, income tax brackets can be found at: http://obliviousinvestor.com/2018-tax-brackets/

Because of this "tax-deduction-now, taxable-withdrawals-later" structure, traditional IRAs are often referred to as "tax-deferred" accounts. The benefit to tax-deferred investing is that your money can grow more quickly than it could if it were taxed on its growth along the way. Even when you account for the fact that it will be taxable when you withdraw it, you still (usually) come out with more after-tax money than you would if you were investing in a taxable brokerage account.

Restrictions on Traditional IRAs

There are restrictions on both the deduction that you get for investing in your IRA and on your ability to withdraw money from your IRA.

First, as of 2018, the annual limit for IRA contributions is the lesser of:

- $5,500 (unless you're 50 or older, in which case you're allowed to contribute up to $6,500), or
- Your taxable compensation for the year.[1]

---

[1] If you're married filing jointly, you can count your spouse's compensation when determining this limit. That is, you and your spouse's *combined* IRA contributions are limited to your *combined* taxable compensation for the year.

Second, if your income reaches a certain level, you may no longer qualify to receive a deduction for the amount that you contribute to your IRA. Specifically, if you are covered by a retirement plan at work (such as a 401(k), which we'll discuss momentarily), your deduction for an IRA contribution will begin to decrease as your modified adjusted gross income for 2018 surpasses:

- $63,000 for single taxpayers, and
- $101,000 for married couples filing jointly.[1]

If your spouse is covered by a retirement plan at work but you are not, your deduction for a traditional IRA contribution begins to decrease once your modified adjusted gross income passes $189,000 for 2018.

If neither you nor your spouse is covered by a retirement plan at work, there is no income limit for the traditional IRA contribution deduction.

The third major restriction on traditional IRAs is that any withdrawals you make before age 59½ will be subject to an extra 10% tax (in addition to being subject to normal income taxes).

---

[1]See IRS Publication 590-A for a definition of modified adjusted gross income:
http://www.irs.gov/publications/p590a/

There are several exceptions to the 59½ rule, however. Specifically, a distribution will not be subject to the additional 10% tax if:

- You are disabled,
- You have died and the distribution is made to your estate or designated beneficiary,
- The distribution does not exceed your medical expense deduction for the year,[1]
- The distribution does not exceed your qualified higher education costs for the year, or
- The distribution is used to buy or build your first home. (Note: Only the first $10,000 of distributions for this purpose will be free from the additional 10% tax.)[2]

Roth IRAs: Tax-Free Distributions

The biggest difference between a traditional IRA and a Roth IRA is that you do *not* get a deduction

---

[1] See the instructions to Schedule A for more about this deduction: https://irs.gov/pub/irs-pdf/i1040sca.pdf

[2] There is another exception for distributions that are part of a "series of substantially equal periodic payments" made over your life expectancy. This can be helpful if you retire early. However, the related rules are rather complex, so consulting a tax professional is a very good idea if you plan to use this exception.

for contributions to a Roth IRA. Instead, when you take money out of your Roth IRA, it will be tax-free. Even the earnings on your contributions come out free of tax.

Restrictions on Roth IRAs

Roth IRAs share the same contribution limits as traditional IRAs. That is, for 2018 you can contribute the lesser of:

- $5,500 ($6,500 if you're age 50 or over), or
- The total of your taxable compensation for the year.

Also, your eligibility to contribute to a Roth IRA is reduced (and eventually eliminated) as your income increases. For 2018:

- For single taxpayers, the amount you can contribute to a Roth IRA begins to decrease as your modified adjusted gross income surpasses $120,000.
- For married taxpayers filing jointly, the amount you can contribute to a Roth IRA begins to decrease as your modified adjusted gross income surpasses $189,000.

As with traditional IRAs, distributions from a Roth IRA made prior to age 59½ are subject to a 10% tax unless they meet certain exceptions. There are, however, two significant differences:

- Contributions (as opposed to earnings on the contributions) can come out free of tax and free of penalty at any time.
- In addition to meeting one of the listed exceptions, distributions of earnings must be made at least 5 years after the first day of the calendar year in which you made your first Roth IRA contribution in order to avoid being subject to income tax.

401(k) Plans

A 401(k) plan—named after subsection 401(k) of the tax code—is a retirement plan through which an employee can choose to have some of her wages/salary deposited into a tax-deferred investment account.[1] In other words, having a 401(k) is a lot like having a traditional IRA provided by your employer. There are, however, several note-

---

[1] 403(b) plans are the comparable plans typically offered by not-for-profit employers. For the purposes of our discussion, the differences between the two are minimal.

worthy differences between 401(k) accounts and IRAs.[1]

Investing via Your 401(k)

401(k) accounts have much higher contribution limits than IRAs. If you are under age 50, your 401(k) contribution limit is $18,500 for 2018. If you are 50 or over, your contribution limit for 2018 is $24,500.

The other primary advantage of 401(k) accounts over IRAs is that, in many cases, employers will "match" employee contributions to the account (up to a certain limit).

EXAMPLE: Your employer matches employee 401(k) contributions up to 4% of the employee's compensation. If your salary is $50,000, your employer will contribute $2,000 (4% of $50,000) to your 401(k) as long as you contribute at least $2,000 over the course of the year.

---

[1] If you're self-employed, rather than having a 401(k) plan at work, you have access to several additional types of retirement plans. For more information, see: http://obliviousinvestor.com/sep-vs-simple-vs-solo-401k/

There are, however, two primary drawbacks of 401(k) accounts as compared to IRAs. First, the investment options in your 401(k) are limited to a pre-selected group of mutual funds. Sometimes this isn't a problem. Unfortunately, many investors are stuck with funds that charge unreasonably high costs. (And as we'll see in Chapter 6, minimizing costs is of the utmost importance when investing.)

Second, your 401(k) administrator—usually a large brokerage firm or fund company—may charge you an administrative fee in addition to the costs paid for the mutual funds. Over time, these costs can eat into your returns significantly.

401(k) Distributions

Like IRA distributions, distributions from a 401(k) will be subject to an additional 10% tax if you are under age 59½. There are, however, some exceptions. Specifically, distributions before age 59½ will not be subject to the additional 10% tax if:

- You are disabled,
- You have died and the distribution is made to your estate or designated beneficiary,
- The distribution does not exceed your medical expense deduction for the year, or

- You have experienced a "separation from service" and the separation occurred during or after the calendar year in which you reached age 55.[1]

Roth 401(k) Accounts

Today, many employers offer a Roth option within their 401(k) plans. Roth 401(k) accounts share a combined contribution limit with regular 401(k) accounts, so the *total* amount you can contribute is limited to $18,500 for 2018 ($24,500 if you're 50 or older).

A Roth 401(k) functions somewhat like a Roth IRA. That is, contributions to a Roth 401(k) do not reduce your taxable income, and distributions from a Roth 401(k) are not subject to income tax, provided that they occur:

1. After you have reached age 59½ (or died or become disabled), and

---

[1] As with IRA distributions, there is an exception to the 10% penalty for early 401(k) distributions that are part of a "series of substantially equal periodic payments" made over your life expectancy. But, again, the rules are complex, and it is best to speak with a tax professional if you want to take advantage of this exception.

2. At least 5 years after the first day of the calendar year in which you first made a Roth contribution to the plan.

If you take any distributions from a Roth 401(k) prior to satisfying those two requirements, the portion of the distribution that represents earnings (rather than contributions you made to the account) will be taxable as income and potentially subject to a 10% additional tax.

Which Account Should I Invest in?

Of course, the big question most investors have is, "Which should I invest in: my 401(k) or an IRA?" Generally speaking, the priority for retirement investing is as follows:

1) Invest enough in your 401(k) (either Roth or tax-deferred[1]) to get the maximum match from your employer,

---

[1] With both IRA and 401(k) accounts, the Roth-or-tax-deferred decision is primarily a function of tax rates. If you expect to be in a higher tax bracket when you retire than you're in now, Roth is probably the better choice. If you expect to be in a lower tax bracket when you retire, tax-deferred contributions are likely better.

2) Max out your IRA contribution (Roth or traditional),
3) Go back to your 401(k) and finish maxing that out, then
4) Invest via taxable accounts.

The reasoning behind the order given is as follows:

a) If your employer provides a dollar-for-dollar match, that's an instant 100% return on your investment. This is, quite simply, too good to pass up.
b) After you've gotten the maximum employer match, maxing out your IRA generally makes more sense than maxing out your 401(k) because IRAs can provide you with more investment options at a lower cost.
c) After you've maxed out your IRA, you may as well max out your 401(k), because the tax benefits provided generally outweigh the drawbacks of limited investment options.

401(k) Rollovers

When you leave your job, you can transfer your 401(k) into either an IRA or a 401(k) with your new employer. This transfer is known as a 401(k) rollover. Rolling over your 401(k) into an IRA is *usually* a good idea, due to the fact that IRAs tend to offer more investment options, at a lower cost.[1]

Chapter 2 Simple Summary

- Traditional IRAs and 401(k) plans allow you to defer taxation upon your income and upon your investments' earnings, thereby allowing your money to grow more quickly.

- Roth IRAs and Roth 401(k) accounts allow for tax-free growth and distributions, provided certain requirements are met.

- Generally speaking, the order of priority for retirement investing is as follows:

1) Contribute enough to your 401(k) to get any available employer match,
2) Max out your IRA (Roth or traditional),
3) Max out your 401(k), then
4) Invest via taxable accounts.

---

[1] There are, however, some cases in which it makes sense to leave your 401(k) where it is. For a more thorough discussion, see here:
http://obliviousinvestor.com/should-i-rollover-my-401k-into-an-ira/

CHAPTER THREE

Risk and Return

Which of the following investments would you pay more for:

A) A signed contract in which the other party agrees to pay you $1,000 every year, regardless of circumstances, or

B) A verbal agreement in which the other party agrees to pay you $1,000 (give or take a few hundred dollars) every year, provided that it won't put too large a strain on his budget?

If you're like most people, you'd pay significantly more for the first investment. Reliable income is more valuable than unreliable income.

Let's say that you decide to purchase both investments. You pay $16,000 for Investment A and $10,000 for Investment B. If both investments do, in fact, end up paying $1,000 for the first year, your rate of return for each investment would be as follows:

Investment A: 6.25% (or $1,000 ÷ $16,000)
Investment B: 10% (or $1,000 ÷ $10,000).

In short, Investment B was riskier (because you were less certain that you'd be paid), but—because you paid less for it—it ended up earning a greater rate of return than Investment A.

How Does This Apply to Real Life?

A similar scenario to the one above plays out on a very large scale in financial markets. Generally, investors are willing to pay more money for predictable income (like that from bonds) than they are for unpredictable income (like that from stocks).

Because investors pay less for unpredictable income, investments that provide unpredictable income should (over time) earn a greater rate of return than investments that provide predictable income—just like in the example above.

In other words, greater risk should mean greater reward (i.e., greater rates of return). This is why, as you can see in the following figure, stocks have historically earned a greater rate of return over extended periods than bonds have.

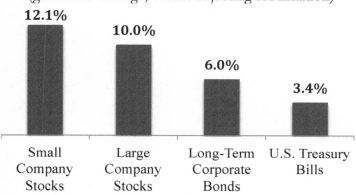

Average Annual Returns 1926-2016
(geometric average, before adjusting for inflation)

Data source: *2017 Stocks, Bonds, Bills, and Inflation (SBBI) Yearbook*

It's Called "Risk" for a Reason.

It is, however, completely untrue to say that high-risk investments *always* outperform low-risk investments. They don't. High-risk investments are high-risk because they're unpredictable. You can't count on them to outperform safer invest-ments over any particular period. Nor can you count on them not to lose money over any particu-lar period.

For the most part though, the likelihood of risky investments outperforming safer investments increases as we look at longer and longer periods.

However, if we're comparing *one* stock to *one* bond, it's quite possible that no matter how long a period we look at, the stock will never outperform the bond. Why? Because with one single stock, anything can happen. The company can even go out of business, sending the stock price permanently to zero.

Therefore, a more accurate statement of the relationship between risk and reward would be to say that a large, diversified group of high-risk investments is likely to outperform a large, diversified group of lower-risk investments. Also, the likelihood of a diversified group of high-risk investments outperforming a diversified group of lower-risk investments increases as we look at longer and longer periods.

For example, the following table shows how frequently the U.S. stock market earned higher returns than 5-year U.S. Treasury bonds over periods of various lengths from 1926 to 2016. However, when looking at the table, it's important to remember that this is just historical data. It's not a prediction of the future. We don't know that stocks will *always* earn more than bonds over 25-year periods (or periods of any specific length, for that matter).

Stocks vs. Treasury Bonds (1926-2016)

How often did stocks earn more than bonds over...

1-Year Periods	59 out of 91	65%
3-Year Periods	66 out of 89	74%
5-Year Periods	63 out of 87	72%
10-Year Periods	67 out of 82	82%
25-Year Periods	67 out of 67	100%

Chapter 3 Simple Summary

- Investors are willing to pay more to obtain reliable sources of income than they are to obtain unreliable sources of income.

- As a result, risky (i.e., unpredictable) investments tend to earn greater rates of return over long periods than less risky (i.e., more predictable) investments.

- The likelihood of a diversified group of high-risk investments outperforming a diversified group of low-risk investments increases as we look at longer periods of time.

CHAPTER FOUR

How to Know
How Much You Need

An integral part of your investment plan is having a firm grasp on what, exactly, you're shooting for. For most people, the primary saving/investing goal is retirement. Too many investors, however, have little idea of how to calculate the amount of money they'll need to have saved up before they can retire.

No method—no matter how sophisticated—will tell you the precise amount of savings that you need in order to be able to retire. There are simply too many unknowable variables. However, getting a very rough estimate doesn't have to be difficult. In fact, you can do it in just two steps.

Step one: Determine Your Spending Needs

The first step is to determine how much you will have to spend from your portfolio each year during retirement. A good starting point for analysis is to take your current annual spending and adjust either upward or downward based on several variables. For example:

- Will your "fun" spending increase due to having more free time? (For example, do you plan to do significantly more traveling than you do now?)
- Will you be finished paying off the mortgage on your home by the time you retire?
- Will you be finished supporting your children? Or will you still be helping to pay for their college education, for instance?
- Will you have to help support your parents or other family members financially?
- How is your health now? Do you have a family history of health problems?

It's important to remember, however, that we're only concerned with how much you will have to spend *from your portfolio* each year. In other words, after getting a ballpark estimate of your *total* annual spending, you'll want to subtract any portion of that spending that you expect to be covered by other sources of income (e.g. pension, Social Security, or a part-time job).

Step 2: Multiply by 25

After estimating the amount of spending that your portfolio will have to satisfy per year, multiply that number by 25. The product is the approximate amount (in today's dollars) that you'll want to have saved before you retire.

We multiply by 25 because multiple studies have shown that, based on historical U.S. market returns, a starting withdrawal rate of more than 4% per year has led to an undesirably high likelihood of running out of money over the course of a 30-year retirement.[1] (And, in order to spend no more than 4% in the first year of retirement, you'll want your portfolio to be at least 25-times the amount that you expect to have to withdraw each year.)

It's important to remember, however, that the future won't look exactly like the past. So

---

[1] One of the better-known studies on the topic is the so-called "Trinity Study," performed by three professors at Trinity University. The full title of the paper is "Retirement Savings: Choosing a Withdrawal Rate That Is Sustainable."

there's certainly no guarantee that a portfolio equal to 25-times your annual spending needs will be large enough to fund your entire retirement.

What About Inflation?

The above process gives you an estimate of how much you would need *in today's dollars* in order to satisfy your desired level of retirement spending. Of course, if you're a long way from retirement, the actual amount necessary will probably be much greater due to inflation.

Unfortunately, there's no way to calculate in advance what the actual dollar requirement will be, because there's no way to know what rate of inflation we'll experience. Fortunately, by revisiting this process every couple of years (i.e., redoing the math using your most recent annual spending as the new starting point), you will automatically be adjusting appropriately for both inflation and changes to your lifestyle. As a result, your estimate will get better and better as you actually near retirement age.

Chapter 4 Simple Summary

- There's no way to determine *precisely* how much money you'll need in order to retire. No matter how sophisticated your analysis, it simply can't be done.

- A very rough estimate of the amount you'll need saved (in today's dollars) in order to retire can be obtained by first estimating how much you'll want to spend from your portfolio each year in retirement, then multiplying by 25.

- It is important to revisit this process periodically in order to adjust your goal for inflation and changes to your lifestyle.

PART TWO

Constructing a Portfolio

CHAPTER FIVE

Don't Bother Picking Stocks.

There's a common belief in our culture that investment success is a function of a person's ability to successfully pick winning stocks. Fortunately, that idea is absolute nonsense. You *do not* need to pick stocks in order to be a successful investor. And, more likely than not, attempting to pick stocks will only harm your returns.

Why Not Pick Stocks?

Every time you buy or sell a stock, there must be somebody, somewhere, on the other side of the transaction (buying the stock if you're selling it, or selling it if you're buying it). Essentially, if you're the buyer, you're betting that the stock will earn an *above* average return in the future, and the seller is betting that the stock is going to earn a *below* average return in the future.

What so many individual investors seem not to understand is that the person on the other side of the transaction is, more likely than not, a professional investor (e.g., the manager of a mutual fund, pension fund, endowment fund, etc.). If you're honest with yourself, how likely is it that you're better informed about the stock in question than a full-time investment professional who has access to expensive research and financial software? As William Bernstein put it in his book *The Four Pillars of Investing*, "You have as much chance of consistently beating these folks as you have of starting at wide receiver for the Broncos."

Invest in Mutual Funds Instead

Rather than attempting to pick stocks on your own, I'd strongly recommend that you invest in low-cost mutual funds. (We'll discuss how to choose among mutual funds in the next chapter.)

Investing in diversified mutual funds frees you from having to constantly watch (and worry about) a portfolio made up of a handful of stocks, as no single stock will make up a significant portion of your mutual fund portfolio.

Also, if you select your mutual funds properly, you can reduce your investment costs significantly, as you'll no longer be paying brokerage commissions to buy and sell stocks all the time. And as we'll discuss more thoroughly later, minimizing the costs associated with your portfolio is one of the most reliable ways to improve your return.

Finally, investing via mutual funds puts you in a position to succeed without having to outsmart the legions of professional investors with whom you're competing when you pick stocks.

But They Told Me It Was Easy!

So why do so many investors make the mistake of thinking that picking above-average stocks will be easy? I suspect that it has a great deal to do with the fact that we've been told precisely that.

After all, there's a lot of money to be made in selling stock tip newsletters, stock-picking software, and so on. Similarly, it's no accident that the biggest financial magazines regularly have articles promoting "5 Hot Stocks You *Need* In Your Portfolio." It's the investment industry's version of "5 Hot Things You *Need* to Try in the Bedroom." It's garbage. But it sure sells magazines!

Chapter 5 Simple Summary

- When you pick stocks, you're competing against full-time, professional investors who have research and analysis resources that you can only dream of. Odds of success: not so good.

- Mutual funds can help minimize your risk by spreading your investment across numerous stocks and bonds.

- When properly chosen, mutual funds can significantly reduce your investment costs, which is one of the most reliable ways to increase your returns.

- Just because a credible-sounding source says that picking stocks is easy doesn't necessarily mean that's the case. Often, when somebody tells you that, they're just trying to sell you something.

CHAPTER SIX

Index Funds Win.

Pay less for a product or service, and you'll have more money left over afterwards. Pretty straightforward, right? For some reason, many investors seem to think that this rule doesn't apply to the field of investing. Big mistake.

Index Funds 101

To recap from Chapter 1: Most mutual funds are run by people picking stocks (or other invest-ments) that they think will earn above-average returns. Index funds, however, are passively managed. That is, they seek only to *match* (rather than beat) the performance of a given index.

For example, index funds could be used to track the performance of:

- The entire U.S. stock market,
- Certain sectors of the U.S. stock market (the pharmaceutical industry, for instance),
- Various international stock markets,
- The bond market of a given country, or
- Just about anything else you can think of.

Most Actively Managed Funds Lose.

The goal of most actively managed funds is to earn a return greater than that of their respective indexes. For example, actively managed U.S. stock funds seek to outperform the return of the U.S. stock market. After all, if an active fund doesn't beat its index, then its investors would have been better off in an index fund that simply tracks the market's return.

Interestingly, most investors actually *would* be better off in index funds. Why? Because, due to the high costs of active management, the majority of actively managed funds fail to outperform their respective indexes. In fact, according to a study done by Standard and Poors, for the ten-year period ending 6/30/2017:

- Less than 15% of U.S. stock funds managed to outperform their respective indexes,

- Less than 21% of international stock funds managed to outperform their respective indexes, and
- Less than 23% of taxable bond funds managed to outperform their respective indexes.[1]

Now, lest you think that this particular period was an anomaly, let me assure you: It wasn't. Standard and Poors has been doing this study since 2002, and each of the studies has shown very similar results. Actively managed funds have failed in both up markets and down markets. They've failed in both domestic markets and international markets. And they've failed in both stock markets and bond markets.

Why Index Funds Win

The investments included in a given index are generally published openly, thereby making it easy for an index fund to track its respective index. (All the fund has to do is buy all of the stocks—or other investments—that are included in the index.) As you can imagine, implementing such a strategy can

---

[1] The study is available at:
http://us.spindices.com/spiva/#/reports

be done at a far lower cost than that charged by the average actively managed fund.

Common sense (and elementary school arithmetic) tells us that:

- If the entire stock market earns, say, a 9% annual return over a given decade, and
- The average dollar invested in the stock market incurs investment costs (such as brokerage commissions and mutual fund fees) of 1.5%,[1]

...then the average dollar invested in the stock market must have earned a net return of 7.5%.

Now, what if you had invested in an index fund that simply sought to *match* the market's return, while incurring only minimal expenses of, say, 0.2%? You would have earned a return of 8.8%, and you would have come out ahead of most other investors.

It's counterintuitive to think that by *not* attempting to outperform the market, an investor can actually come out above average. But it's completely true. The math is indisputable. John Bogle (the founder of Vanguard and the creator of

---

[1] According to the Investment Company Institute, the average expense ratio for a stock mutual fund in 2016 was 1.28%.

the first index fund) refers to this phenomenon as "The Relentless Rules of Humble Arithmetic."[1]

Why Not Pick a Hot Fund?

Naturally, many investors are inclined to ask, "Why not invest in an actively managed fund that *does* beat its index?" In short: because it's hard— far harder than most would guess—to predict ahead of time which actively managed funds will be the top performers.

In addition to their "indices versus active" scorecards, Standard and Poors also puts out "persistence scorecards" from time to time.[2] In the most recent one (published June 2017), they found that of the funds that had a top-quartile ranking for the five years ending March 2012, only 22.43% maintained a top-quartile ranking for the following five-year period. Pure randomness would suggest a repeat rate of 25%. In other words, picking funds based on superior past performance proved to be no better than picking randomly!

In another study, Morningstar's Russel Kinnel looked at the usefulness of expense ratios and star ratings (which are based on past perfor-

---

[1] See: *The Little Book of Common Sense Investing*

[2] Available at: http://us.spindices.com/resource-center/thought-leadership/research/

mance) at predicting future performance.[1] Kinnel summarized his findings:

> Investors should make expense ratios a primary test in fund selection. They are still the most dependable predictor of performance. [...] Stars can be helpful, too, particularly in identifying funds that might be merged out of existence.

In other words, past performance can be useful for identifying future *poor* performers. (That is, the worst performing funds tend to continue to perform poorly, and they are often shut down by the fund company running them.) But if you're looking to pick a future *top* performer, picking a low-cost fund is your best bet. And looking for low-cost funds naturally leads to the selection of index funds as likely top-performers.

Taxes Are Costs Too.

If you're investing in a taxable account (as opposed to a 401(k) or IRA), index funds can help you not only to minimize costs, but to minimize taxes as well. With mutual funds, you pay taxes each year

---

[1] Kinnel's article about the study can be found here: http://news.morningstar.com/articlenet/article.aspx?id=347327

on your share of the capital gains realized within the fund's portfolio.

Because most active fund managers buy and sell investments so rapidly,[1] a large percentage of the gains end up being short-term capital gains.[2] Because short-term capital gains are taxed at your ordinary income tax rate (as opposed to long-term capital gains, which are taxed at a maximum rate of 20%), you'll end up paying more taxes with actively managed funds than you would with index funds, which typically hold on to their investments for longer periods of time.

Not All Index Funds Are Low-Cost.

Do not, however, invest in a fund simply because it's an index fund. Some index funds actually charge expense ratios that are close to—or sometimes even above—those charged by actively

---

[1] According to the Investment Company Institute's 2017 Investment Company Fact Book, in 2016 stock mutual funds turned over more than a third (34%) of their respective portfolios during the year. And that calculation included index funds, which tend to have low turnover. In other words, most actively managed stock funds have *very* high turnover.

[2] Short-term capital gains are those incurred when an investment is sold for a gain after being held for one year or less.

managed funds. It's a good idea to take the time to check a fund's expense ratio (and compare it to the expense ratios of other funds in the same category) before investing in it.[1]

When Index Funds Aren't an Option

Unfortunately, in many investors' primary retirement account—their 401(k) or 403(b)—they don't have the option to select any low-cost index funds. If you find yourself in such a situation, my strategy for picking funds would be as follows:

1) Determine your ideal overall asset allocation (that is, how much of your overall portfolio you want invested in U.S. stocks, how much in international stocks, and how much in bonds).[2]
2) Determine which of your fund options could be used for each piece of your asset allocation.

---

[1] Information regarding expense ratios will be easy to find in a fund's prospectus, on the fund company's website, or on Morningstar.com.

[2] Determining your ideal asset allocation is the topic of Chapter 7.

3) Among those funds, choose the ones with the lowest expense ratios and the lowest portfolio turnover.[1]

Chapter 6 Simple Summary

• Because of their low costs, index funds consistently outperform the majority of their actively managed competitors.

• A fund's past performance (even over extended periods) is *not* a reliable way to predict future performance.

• Not all index funds are low-cost. Before investing in an index fund, take the time to compare its expense ratio to the expense ratios of other index funds in the same category (e.g., international equity index funds).

• If you don't have access to low-cost index funds in your retirement plan at work, look for low-cost, low-turnover funds that fit your desired asset allocation.

---

[1] Portfolio turnover refers to the percentage of a fund's portfolio that is sold over the course of the year. Higher turnover means higher costs, and these costs are not included in the fund's published expense ratio.

CHAPTER SEVEN

Asset Allocation
and Risk Tolerance

So far, in terms of constructing a portfolio, we've determined that:

a) There's little sense in attempting to pick individual stocks and bonds rather than investing in mutual funds, and
b) When it comes to selecting mutual funds, low-cost index funds are your best bet.

The next piece of the portfolio construction puzzle is asset allocation: How much of your portfolio should be invested in each asset class (e.g., U.S. stocks, international stocks, and bonds)?

Your tolerance for risk is the most important factor in determining an appropriate asset allocation. The primary factors determining your risk tolerance are:

1) The degree of flexibility you have with regard to your financial goals, and
2) Your personal comfort level with volatility in your portfolio.

EXAMPLE 1: Jason is a construction worker. He's 57, and each day he is becoming increasingly aware that his body is unlikely to be able to continue in his line of work for more than two or three more years. Between his Social Security and savings, Jason is pretty sure that his basic expenses will be covered—but only barely. Because Jason can neither delay his retirement nor reduce his expenses, Jason has a low ability to take risk.

EXAMPLE 2: Debbie is 54. She hopes to retire at 62 with enough savings to provide for $50,000 of annual spending. Debbie likes her work though, so she wouldn't terribly mind having to work until her late 60s. And $50,000 is just a goal. She knows she could get by just fine with about 70% of that. Because Debbie's goals are flexible, she has a greater ability to take risk.

Your risk tolerance is also affected by your comfort level with volatility. One way to estimate this comfort level is to ask yourself, "How far could my portfolio fall before I started losing sleep, feeling stressed, or wanting to sell everything and move to cash?"

When answering this question, be sure to answer both as a percentage *and as a dollar value*—otherwise you may come to inaccurate conclusions. For example, you may remember that at age 25 you experienced a 40% loss and handled it just fine. But if you're 45 now, and your portfolio is 10-times the size that it was at age 25, a 40% loss could be an entirely different experience.

When assessing your risk tolerance, it's generally wise to guess conservatively. If you end up with a portfolio that's slightly too conservative for your tastes, you'll only be missing out on a relatively small incremental return.

In contrast, if you end up with a portfolio that's too aggressive, you might end up panicking during periods of high volatility. Even one instance of getting out of the market after a sharp decline can be more than enough to eliminate the extra return you were hoping to earn from having a stock-heavy allocation.

Stocks vs. Bonds

Once you have an idea of your risk tolerance level, it's time to move on to the first (and most important) part of the asset allocation decision: your stock/bond allocation.

One rule of thumb that serves as a reasonable starting point for analysis is to consider limiting your stock allocation to the maximum tolerable loss that you determined above, times two. Or, said differently, assume that your stocks can lose 50% of their value at any time.

The most important thing to remember with asset allocation guidelines, however, is that they're just that: guidelines. For example, with regard to this particular rule of thumb, it's important to understand that a loss greater than 50% certainly *could* occur, despite the fact that such declines are historically uncommon. This is especially true if your stock holdings are not well diversified or if your non-stock holdings are high-risk such that they could decline significantly in value at the same time that your stocks do.

U.S. Stocks vs. International Stocks

It's not terribly surprising to learn that the U.S. stock market isn't the best performing market in the world every single year. In fact, it's often not in the top 10.

The difficulty in international investing—as with picking stocks or actively managed mutual funds—is that it's nearly impossible to know ahead of time *which* countries are going to have the best market performance over a given time period. The solution? Own each (or at least many) of them.

The primary goal of investing a portion of your portfolio internationally should not be to increase returns, as there is no guarantee that international markets will outperform our own. Rather, the primary goal is to increase the diversification of your portfolio, thereby reducing your risk.

In total, the U.S. stock market makes up roughly half of the value of all of the publicly traded stocks in the world. However, most investment professionals recommend allocating more than 50% of the stock portion of your portfolio to domestic equities. Why? Because investing internationally introduces an additional type of risk into your portfolio: currency risk.

Currency risk is the risk that your return from investing in international stocks will be reduced as a result of the U.S. dollar increasing in value relative to the value of the currencies of the countries in which you have invested.

EXAMPLE: A portion of your portfolio is invested in Japanese stocks, and over the next year it earns a return of 8%. However, over that same period, the value of the yen relative to the dollar decreases by 3%. Your annual return (as measured in dollars) would only be roughly 5%.

So how much of your portfolio should be invested internationally? There's a great deal of debate on this issue, with investment professionals recommending a very wide range of international allocations.

The trick is that without knowing how the U.S. market will perform in comparison to markets abroad, there's simply no way to know what the "best" allocation will be. In my own opinion, allocating anywhere from 20% to 40% of the stock portion of your portfolio to international index funds would be reasonable for most investors.[1]

Rebalancing

No matter how perfectly you craft your portfolio, there's little doubt that in not too terribly long, your asset allocation will be (to use a technical term) out of whack. The stock market will have either shot upward, thereby causing your stock allocation to be higher than intended, or it will have experienced a downturn, causing your stock allocation to be lower than intended.

Rebalancing is the act of adjusting your holdings to bring them back in line with your ideal asset allocation. A periodic rebalancing program

---

[1] See the following study from Vanguard for a more thorough explanation of this recommended range of international allocations:
https://personal.vanguard.com/pdf/icriecr.pdf

helps keep the risk level of your portfolio in line with your goals.[1]

How often should an investor rebalance? That's a tricky question. Some people advocate in favor of rebalancing once your portfolio is off balance by a certain amount, such as your stock allocation being either 10% higher or 10% lower than intended. Others argue that rebalancing should be done at regular intervals—annually on your birthday for instance—regardless of how off-balance your portfolio becomes in the interim.

Unfortunately, the best-performing rebalancing strategy varies from period to period, and it's no easy task to predict which strategy will do best over the course of *your* investing career. Rather than spending a great deal of time and effort thinking about it, my suggestion is simply to pick one method and resolve to stick with it.

---

[1] It's worth noting that rebalancing can be *extremely* difficult emotionally/psychologically. It can feel as if you're selling your "good investments" to put money into your "bad investments." The key is to remember that just because something has performed well (or poorly) recently doesn't mean that it will continue to do so in the immediate future.

Chapter 7 Simple Summary

- Your tolerance for risk should be the primary determinant of your stock/bond allocation. Your risk tolerance is determined by how comfortable you are with investment volatility and how flexible your financial goals are.

- Generally speaking, it's better to have an asset allocation that's too conservative than an asset allocation that's too aggressive.

- For the sake of additional diversification, most investment professionals recommend investing somewhere from 20% to 40% of your stock holdings internationally.

- Rebalancing is the act of bringing your portfolio back to its targeted asset allocation (and, therefore, its targeted risk level).

CHAPTER EIGHT

Putting the Pieces Together

So what, exactly, might a diversified, low-cost index fund portfolio look like? Such a portfolio can be constructed using just three index funds. For example, at Vanguard, such a portfolio might include the following funds:

1) Vanguard Total Stock Market Index Fund (for the U.S. stock portion of your portfolio),
2) Vanguard Total International Stock Index Fund (for the international stock portion of your portfolio), and
3) Vanguard Total Bond Market Index Fund (for the bond portion of your portfolio).

Alternatively, a very similar low-cost portfolio could be put together at Fidelity using their index funds:

1) Fidelity Total Market Index Fund,
2) Fidelity International Index Fund, and
3) Fidelity U.S. Bond Index Fund.

There's little need to complicate things beyond that. In either case, your portfolio would be extremely diversified, consisting of more than a thousand investment-grade bonds and thousands of stocks from several different countries. And you would be doing an excellent job of minimizing your investment costs. As of this writing, each of the funds mentioned above has an expense ratio of 0.18% or less.

Looking for Something More Sophisticated?

My experience tells me that, while many investors will find the simplicity of the above portfolios to be a tremendous relief, others will find it unsatisfying. Some investors have a desire for a portfolio that feels sophisticated. If that's you, the following are a few changes you could make that won't add too much complexity and that could potentially improve your results.

First, you may want to consider substituting a fund that invests in Treasury Inflation-Protected Securities (TIPS) for a portion of your bond holdings. TIPS are bonds issued by the federal government that protect investors from inflation by promising a certain after-inflation return.[1]

A second potential modification would be to adjust the portfolio to slightly overweight small-cap stocks and/or value stocks, as a considerable amount of research has shown that small-cap stocks tend to have greater returns than large-cap stocks and that value stocks tend to have greater returns than growth stocks.[2] It should be noted, however, that value stocks and small-cap stocks are known to carry higher levels of risk than their counterparts (hence the greater expected returns).

Finally, you may find it desirable to overweight real estate investment trusts (REITs).[3] Because they tend to have a low correlation to the rest of the stock market, REITs might offer an

---

[1] As opposed to most bonds, which offer a specific before-inflation (i.e., "nominal") return. More information about TIPS can be found at:

treasurydirect.gov/indiv/products/prod_tips_glance.htm

[2] Value stocks being those that trade at low prices relative to various measures of fundamental value (most frequently earnings per share or book value per share).

[3] I say "overweight" because REITs are already included in a typical "total stock market" index fund.

additional level of diversification, thereby potentially reducing the overall risk of your portfolio.

For example, somebody implementing each of the above adjustments in a Vanguard account might end up with the following funds (among which she would allocate based on her risk tolerance):

1) Vanguard Total Stock Market Index Fund,
2) Vanguard Total International Stock Index Fund,
3) Vanguard Total Bond Market Index Fund,
4) Vanguard Small-Cap Value Index Fund,
5) Vanguard REIT Index Fund, and
6) Vanguard Inflation-Protected Securities Fund.

Chapter 8 Simple Summary

- After determining an appropriate asset allocation, you can construct an extremely well diversified, low-cost portfolio using just a few index funds.

Exchange-Traded Funds (ETFs)

Exchange Traded Funds (ETFs) are investments that, like traditional mutual funds, own other investments. And, for the most part, ETFs are like index funds in that they're passively managed (usually tracking a given index, just like an index fund) and they offer a low-cost way to invest. *Unlike* traditional mutual funds, however, ETFs are bought and sold like regular stocks.

Comparing Expenses

Several years ago, arguably the biggest factors in the decision of whether to use traditional index funds or ETFs were that ETFs had slightly lower expense ratios than most index funds, but you had to pay a commission to purchase them (as you would to purchase any stock).

Over the last several years, however, multiple brokerage firms (including Vanguard, Fidelity, Schwab, and TD Ameritrade) have begun to allow for commission-free trades of certain low-cost ETFs. On the other hand, ETFs no longer offer much (if anything) in the way of savings with regard to expense ratios. Today, the lowest-cost index funds have expense ratios that are comparable to the lowest-cost ETFs.

In short, when it comes to expenses, there is no longer a significant difference between the lowest-cost ETFs and the lowest-cost index funds. For example, the following low-cost, diversified ETF portfolio could be purchased commission-free at Schwab and would have very similar expense ratios to a comparable index fund (or ETF) portfolio at Vanguard or Fidelity:

1) Schwab U.S. Broad Market ETF,
2) Schwab International Equity ETF, and
3) Schwab U.S. Aggregate Bond ETF.

More Important Considerations

For most investors, the ETF vs. index fund decision comes down to considerations other than costs. It makes sense to use ETFs if you care about things that are only possible because of the fact that they trade like stocks—things like:

- Buying or selling your holdings in the middle of the day,
- Buying on margin (that is, investing with money borrowed from your brokerage firm), or
- Using types of orders other than market orders (limit orders, for instance, in which you would tell your brokerage firm to buy or sell a certain number of shares if/when the price per share falls below, or rises above, a certain point).

Conversely, it makes sense to use traditional index funds if you care about:

- Being able to buy fractional shares, or
- Setting up automatic purchases (or sales) at regular intervals.

Personally, I couldn't care less about the particular advantages offered by ETFs, but I *do* care about the ability to set up automatic purchases. As a result, I prefer to use traditional index funds. For other investors, ETFs will be a better fit.

In any case, for investors using a "buy, hold, and rebalance" strategy, the differences between low-cost ETFs and low-cost index funds are slim.[1] Your long-term success is unlikely to be affected either way as a result of the decision.

Chapter 9 Simple Summary

- Most ETFs are essentially index funds that trade like stocks.

- In recent years, multiple brokerage firms have begun to offer commission-free trades on certain ETFs. At the same time, the expense ratios on traditional index funds have decreased. As a result, there's no longer a large difference in costs between the lowest-cost ETFs and the lowest-cost index funds.

---

[1] I specify "low-cost" ETFs because, like index funds, there are many with unreasonably high costs.

CHAPTER TEN

Target Date Funds

One of the biggest developments in the field of investing in recent years is the invention of the target date fund. Target date funds (usually named something like "Retirement 2030") are funds that automate your asset allocation and rebalancing program for you. They do this by holding shares of other mutual funds and adjusting your stock allocation downward over time (as the named retirement date approaches).

Unfortunately, as great as the target date fund concept is, the implementation has left a lot to be desired. For example, many target date funds invest in high-cost actively managed funds rather than low-cost index funds. Further, some target date funds charge an extra level of expenses in addition to those charged by the funds owned by the target date fund—a sure strategy for subpar results.

Two companies that do offer low-cost, passive target date funds are Vanguard (with their Vanguard Target Retirement lineup) and Fidelity (with their Fidelity Freedom Index Fund lineup).[1] In addition, some employer-sponsored retirement plans (most notably, the Thrift Savings Plan available to federal government employees) provide access to low-cost target date funds that are not available to retail investors.

Target Date Fund Drawbacks

Of course, these funds have their drawbacks too. First, if your portfolio is large enough, you could often achieve *slightly* lower expenses by using individual index funds or ETFs.

Second, for investors in taxable accounts, target date funds could be less tax-efficient than a portfolio made up of separate funds. For example, an investor in a high tax bracket could benefit from using tax-exempt municipal bonds rather than the taxable bonds included in a target date fund.

---

[1] Caution: It's easy to confuse Fidelity Freedom *Index* Funds with the similarly named Fidelity Freedom Funds. The Fidelity Freedom Funds are also target date funds, but they have much higher costs (approximately four times as high as of this writing) due to their use of active mutual funds.

Finally, there's no guarantee that the fund company will stick to the planned asset allocation glide path. That is, the current plan may be for the fund to have a certain allocation 15 years from now, but the fund company can change that plan at any time. As a result, an investor who pays no attention could end up with a different allocation than he/she had anticipated.

Pick Based on Risk

If you decide to use a target date fund, do not pick solely based on the date in the name. Instead, take the time to look at the funds' respective asset allocations, and pick the one that is the best fit for you. You may find that the fund that best fits your own tolerance for risk is the one typically intended for investors retiring 10 or 20 years earlier or later than you.

Chapter 10 Simple Summary

- Target date funds can be an excellent way to implement a low-maintenance, low-cost, diversified portfolio.

- Before investing in a target date fund, check to make sure that its expenses are reasonable and that its asset allocation is in line with what you feel is appropriate for your needs.

- If you're investing in a taxable account (as opposed to a 401(k) or IRA), target date funds are probably not the most tax-efficient way to invest.

PART THREE

Staying Out of Trouble

CHAPTER ELEVEN

Think Long-Term

If you're investing in the stock market for any extended period of time, there's no question that you'll experience your share of bear markets. Sometimes the declines will be short lived, lasting only a few months. Other times the market will take years to recover. Sometimes the declines will be relatively minor. Other times they'll be frighteningly sudden and severe.

Successful investing does not require you to devise a system of predicting bear markets ahead of time. Successful investing simply requires that you pick an allocation that allows you to respond to these downturns appropriately (by not panicking and selling immediately *after* the downturn).

Isn't That Just Common Sense?

As obvious as it would seem to avoid selling after a downturn, the typical investor tends to have a great deal of trouble keeping himself from doing so. Why? It's a combination of several factors, really.

First, investors take the information that the market has just *gone* down and—without realizing what they're doing—thereby assume that the market will *continue* to go down in the near future. Of course, if predicting the market were really so easy, there would be far more multimillionaires out there.[1]

Second, the financial media has a vested interest in sensationalizing market movements, whether upward or downward. During bear markets, the financial news often borders on fear mongering. This, of course, does little to help investors maintain confidence in their stock market holdings.

Third, when most investors check their portfolios and see that their account values have gone down, they experience psychological stress. After enough "My account is down *again*?" experi-

---

[1] This human tendency to believe that whatever has happened recently will continue to happen in the future is known as "recency bias," and it affects us as much during bull markets as during bear markets.

ences, it's easy to understand why an investor might eventually capitulate and get out of the market just to make the pain stop.

Don't Peek (Very Often).

Aside from choosing an allocation that's appropriate for your risk tolerance, one of the most effective methods of avoiding the temptation to jump out of the market after a downturn is simply to avoid watching the market (and your account value) so closely. It's perfectly reasonable to check your portfolio no more than a handful of times each year.

One of my all-time favorite pieces of investing advice comes courtesy of John Bogle[1]:

> Try and avoid the worst hazards of behavioral investing. Follow the basic rule that I follow: Don't peek. Don't look at your account. Throw the 401(k) statement in the trash when it comes.

If you have a time horizon of several years—and if you don't, you shouldn't have your money in the stock market in the first place—then you don't

---

[1] During an interview with Steve Perlstein from *On Leadership*

have to worry about what goes on in the market from month to month. All you need to be concerned with is what will happen in the market over the next several years (specifically, between now and the time you'll need to take your money out to spend it—most likely during retirement).

Conveniently enough, we have good reason to be confident that the stock market—and thus, an index fund that tracks the entire stock market—will increase in value over any extended period.

Why You Can Be Confident about Owning the Stock Market

Common sense tells us that being the owner of a profitable company is a profitable endeavor. And that's precisely what you're doing when you invest in broadly diversified stock index funds: You're investing in companies so that you can receive a share of their profits.

Is every company profitable? Of course not. However, if you own a portion of each of the publicly traded companies in the United States (as well as a few thousand companies in other countries), you can be confident that, on the whole, those companies will earn a net profit. Over time, that profit will be returned to the shareholders in the form of dividend payments and increases in share values.

Beware of Bull Markets as Well

Just as we're tempted to respond inappropriately to bear markets, so are we tempted to respond inappropriately to bull markets. If the stock market has spent the last few years posting annual returns in excess of 20% (as it did during the second half of the 1990s), it can be *very* tempting to sell your bond funds and move everything into stocks.

In other words, we have a natural human tendency not only to *sell* after a price *decline*, but to *buy* after a price *increase*—precisely the opposite of what we should be doing. Perhaps not surprisingly, the reasons for this urge to "buy high" are analogous to the reasons we're tempted to "sell low." Specifically:

1) We tend to assume that just because the market has been going up lately, it will continue to do so in the immediate future,
2) During bull markets, the financial media works to instigate a stock market mania, and
3) When the market is shooting upward, we derive pleasure from our stock market holdings. It's only natural that we're tempted to buy more.

71

Again, the best way to combat the counterproductive desire to jump in and out of the market is to avoid watching the market so often. Rather than trying to predict the market's next movement, focus instead on maintaining an asset allocation that is appropriate for your risk tolerance and your investment time frame.

Chapter 11 Simple Summary

- To be a successful investor, you do *not* need to be able to predict market declines. You simply need to be able to refrain from bailing out afterwards.

- As easy as it sounds to avoid "selling low," several psychological quirks make it difficult for investors to do so.

- One of the most effective ways to avoid stressing yourself out about your portfolio is simply to check it less frequently.

- Over time, most businesses earn a profit. If you own thousands of businesses for an extended period of time, you can be confident that your holdings will earn a profit as well.

- We're tempted not only to "sell low" during bear markets but also to "buy high" during bull markets. Instead of trying to time the market, do your best to maintain an asset allocation that is appropriate for your risk tolerance.

CHAPTER TWELVE

How to Find a *Good* Financial Advisor

Using the services of a trustworthy, well-informed financial advisor is one of the best things you can do to increase the likelihood of meeting your financial goals. Of course, the flip side is that using a dishonest or poorly informed financial advisor is one of the fastest ways imaginable to make your money disappear.

First things first though...

Do You Need an Advisor?

For many investors, the answer is, "No, you don't need one." Most of the truly important aspects of personal finance can be easily understood by a motivated individual with no more than a high school education. There are, however, cases in which it makes sense to find a professional to help you with your finances. Specifically it may make sense to use a financial advisor if:

- You are not motivated to learn about investing, taxation, budgeting, and so on,
- You're the type who is likely to benefit significantly from having somebody to call and talk things over with when the market is at its most volatile (and therefore most frightening), or
- You are in (or nearing) retirement.

The reason that financial advisors can provide greater value to investors in or nearing retirement is that by the time you're close to retirement, your portfolio is substantial in size. Therefore, mistakes (like an inappropriate asset allocation) are more costly than they've ever been. Also, at age 60 you have less time to make up for mistakes than you did at age 30. In addition, it can be useful to get advice on various retirement planning topics such as when to claim Social Security benefits or which account (Roth IRA, traditional IRA, taxable, etc.) to draw from first.

Commissions? Hourly Fees? Asset-Based Fees?

Once you start researching financial advisors, you'll quickly learn that they charge for their services in one of a few different ways: commissions, hourly fees, and periodic, asset-based fees. Each comes with its own set of pros and cons.

Commission-based advisors can sometimes be the least expensive of the bunch. The drawback is that such a compensation structure creates a significant conflict of interest between the client and the advisor. The advisor will have an incentive to sell you whichever products pay the most commission (typically high-cost mutual funds, or even higher-cost annuities), regardless of what's in *your* interests. Also, commission-based advisors have an incentive to persuade you to buy and sell investments more frequently than you should, as they receive a commission on each transaction.

Other advisors charge a simple hourly fee each time you meet with them. This is wonderful in that it makes for mostly-unbiased advice—the advisor has no incentive to persuade you to do anything other than whatever is in your best interests. The drawback, of course, is that such hourly meetings are often rather pricey, sometimes making them prohibitively expensive for young investors with small portfolios.

The third option is to use an advisor who charges a periodic retainer in exchange for managing your portfolio and meeting with you a certain number of times per year. This fee is usually a percentage of the total amount of assets you have invested. Like hourly fees, this structure allows the advisor to provide you with mostly-unbiased advice. Again, the drawback is that such fees can really add up. A fee equal to 1% of your portfolio each year for several decades is no small sum.

Remember: Index Funds Win.

When interviewing potential financial advisors, make it a point to find one who uses low-cost index funds or ETFs for his/her clients' portfolios. Be *extremely* wary of any claim by a financial advisor that he can reliably pick stocks or funds that will outperform a portfolio of low-cost index funds.

After all, if most fund managers can't beat index funds, why should we believe a financial advisor who claims that he can? Remember, trying to beat the market is a fund manager's full-time job. Financial advisors have to spend time meeting with clients and performing marketing activities to find new clients. Researching stocks and mutual funds is, at best, their third-highest priority.

Chapter 12 Simple Summary

- Most investors do not *need* a financial advisor if they're sufficiently motivated to learn the basics of personal finance and investing.

- The closer you are to retirement, the more value a financial advisor can provide.

- Each of the various compensation structures has its pros and cons. To the extent possible, however, try to ensure that your financial advisor's interests are aligned with your own.

- Don't put too much faith in a financial advisor's claims that he/she can beat the market (even if the advisor has managed to do so in the past). Instead, opt for a financial advisor who understands the wisdom of a buy, hold, and rebalance strategy using low-cost investments.

CHAPTER THIRTEEN

Automate Your Investing

There aren't many things in our lives that we can truly automate. *Somebody* has to make sure the laundry gets washed and the house gets cleaned. And, despite all the talk online about building "passive" income, most people I know still have to get up and go to work in the morning in order to make a living.

Investing is one of the rare exceptions. Aside from some minor maintenance tasks a couple of times each year, your investments can (and should) be completely automated.

Beat Laziness (With No Effort!)

The single most important thing you can do to increase your chance of having enough money to be able to retire someday is to save and invest regularly, year-in and year-out, over a period of multiple decades. The catch, of course, is that between procrastination and forgetfulness, it's extremely unlikely that you'll actually take the time to sign in and transfer money to your brokerage account *every month for 30 years.*

Why not automate your investing instead? The most obvious method is to enroll in your 401(k) plan at work so that you'll have an amount withheld automatically from each of your paychecks.

If, however, you've already maxed out your 401(k), your employer doesn't offer one, or the investment options are particularly lousy, you can achieve the same thing via an IRA. Every major brokerage firm will allow you to have a certain amount withdrawn automatically from your checking account each month and deposited into your IRA. Just tell them how much you want to invest each month and which funds you want it invested in, and you're all set.

Nothing is *Ever* Left Over.

Automating your IRA and 401(k) contributions ensures that you actually invest for your future. In my experience, when investors go about it from the other direction (that is, budgeting their expenditures and then investing whatever is left over), they end up investing nothing. For most people, nothing is *ever* left over. It's most people's natural tendency to spend as much as they have. Why not accept that fact, and make your contributions automatic?

Minimize the Need to Peek

As we discussed in Chapter 11, the more frequently you check your portfolio, the more tempted you'll be to react (usually inappropriately) to short-term market movements. Automating your investments helps you to minimize the frequency with which you check your portfolio.

Chapter 13 Simple Summary

- Plain old procrastination and forgetfulness are two of the biggest hurdles for many investors. Automate your investments, and you'll win that battle easily.

- For most investors, investing what's left over after covering expenses doesn't work. *Nothing* is left over. Instead, automate your investing so that you *save* first, then *spend* what's left over.

- Automating your investments helps to minimize the desire to check your portfolio obsessively, thereby also reducing the likelihood that you'll respond inappropriately to short-term market movements.

CHAPTER FOURTEEN

Beware the Hot Fund

The smartest kid in your 4th grade class was probably the smartest kid in your 5th grade class as well. The best quarterback in the NFL this year is likely to be one of the best next year. The company's top salesperson from this year will probably be near the top next year. You get the idea—in general, top performers continue to be top performers.

So it's no surprise that when we see an ad promoting a mutual fund that has outperformed the market for each of the last seven years, we tend to be impressed. It's reasonable to think that if a guy has done well at his job before, he will probably continue to do well. That's just common sense.

The catch is that it doesn't work that way with mutual funds. Numerous studies have shown that when it comes to mutual funds, past performance is a rather poor indicator of future results.

That is, in fact, why mutual fund advertisements are required to include a disclaimer saying exactly that. If only we could convince ourselves to listen!

Is it Purely Luck?

Let's imagine a hypothetical group of 1,024 actively managed funds. If we look at pre-expense results, roughly 50% of the funds should outperform the market each year. That means that after 7 years:

- Approximately 8 of the funds will have outperformed the market every year,
- Approximately 64 funds will have outperformed the market in at least 6/7 years, and
- Approximately 232 funds will have outperformed the market in at least 5/7 years.

And that's based purely on luck. No need for any fund management skill at all.

According to the Investment Company Institute, at the beginning of 2011, there were 3,259 domestic equity mutual funds.[1] Using our numbers from above, we can see that pure luck would account for approximately 738 different funds outperforming the market in at least 5 of the last 7

---

[1] Data available at: icifactbook.org/data/17_fb_data

years on a pre-expense basis. There would even be roughly 25 funds that would have outperformed in *each* of the last 7 years.

So what does it tell us when a fund has such a record? Not very much. There are so many funds out there that there will *always* be several with superstar performance. Beware of ads suggesting that those fund managers are brilliant or that those funds will continue to beat the market.

When a Company Has Hundreds of Funds...

Some readers may be wondering, "Well what about [some particular company]? I always see their funds promoted as being high performers. How is it possible that they've gotten lucky so consistently?" That's a fair question. Before drawing any conclusions though about the quality of a company's fund managers, be sure to consider the overall *number* of funds that they run. For instance, as of this writing, Fidelity has more than 300 mutual funds. So is it any surprise that they always have several funds whose performance they can advertise?

Further, we'd be wise to take note of the fact that these aren't the only funds that Fidelity has ever operated. It's a common practice throughout the mutual fund industry to shut down funds that consistently underperform their benchmarks. As Larry Swedroe put it in his book *The Successful Investor Today*, it appears that the actively managed fund industry follows the mantra, "If at first you don't succeed, destroy any evidence that you tried."

What about Risk?

Most times, a fund's above-market performance can be explained entirely by luck. Other times, however, the high returns could be the result of the fund manager taking on more risk than other funds.

For example, consider two hypothetical bond funds:

- Fund A is an index fund that tracks the Barclays US Aggregate Bond Index (an index intended to reflect the return of the U.S. bond market), and
- Fund B is an actively managed bond fund.

Let's imagine that Fund A has earned an average annual return of 3% over the last 5 years, and Fund B has earned an average annual return of 4% over the same period. Is Fund B's outperformance due to the skill of the fund manager? That's possible. Is it due purely to luck? That's also possible.

Another possibility, though, is that Fund B is taking on more risk than Fund A by investing in riskier bonds, such as bonds that have been issued by companies with poor credit ratings. As we discussed in Chapter 3, high-risk assets tend to earn higher rates of return than low-risk assets.

The danger, of course, is that those bonds are more likely to go into default than the bonds held by Fund A. If the credit markets were to tighten significantly at some point (like they did in 2008-2009), there's a chance that Fund A would hold up relatively well, while Fund B's value would plummet due to some of its bond holdings going into default.

In short, before attributing a fund manager's superstar performance to skill, take a moment to check what the fund actually owns. You don't want to get caught buying a high-risk fund when you didn't intend to.

What about Recommendations from Unbiased Sources?

Of course, we all know to be skeptical of advertising claims of any sort, so it's hardly a revelation to learn that it's wise to do the same thing with mutual fund ads. What many investors don't pick up on, however, is that the same skepticism should be applied to seemingly unbiased sources (both online and offline).

Just as financial magazines and websites run articles with headlines like "5 Hot Stocks to Buy," they also run articles recommending hot funds (or profiling new superstar fund managers). And, just like the articles about hot stocks, the ones about hot mutual funds are of dubious value.

The financial media naturally benefits from the active management industry because it gives them an unending source of fresh content. There's always some sharp, new fund manager who has handsomely beaten the market for the last few years. Does that mean she'll continue to beat the market? The truth is, from the perspective of the website publishing the article, that's irrelevant. What's relevant is that the headline sounded exciting, got your attention, and got you to click on the article.

Another valuable lesson can be gained from buying a financial magazine and paging through it from cover to cover, counting all the ads for T.Rowe Price, Charles Schwab, Fidelity, and so on. A *very* significant portion of financial magazines' advertising revenue comes from active-management fund companies. It should be no surprise that the magazines are somewhat reluctant to give readers the blunt truth: In most cases, you're better off with boring, low-cost index funds than with actively managed mutual funds.

Chapter 14 Simple Summary

- Due to the huge number of mutual funds in existence, pure luck can account for the fact that there are always several funds with impressive-looking performance records.

- Whether it's an advertisement, an article, or a financial advisor promoting a fund's performance record, do *not* expect the fund to beat the market just because it has done so in the past.

- The most reliable way to pick above-average funds is to pick funds with below-average costs (which usually means index funds or ETFs).

CHAPTER FIFTEEN

Turn Off the Television

Everyday, we're bombarded with news about the stock market. The newspaper tells us when the market hits new highs or lows. The evening and morning news tell us how the Dow Jones Industrial Average, S&P 500, and Nasdaq each performed over the last 24 hours. Stock prices are projected across the bottom of the TV screen—sometimes during programs that have nothing to do with investing or money in general. And information about market movements is a constant presence on news websites and social media.

This flood of information is problematic for two reasons:

1) It convinces investors that we need to pay attention to short-term market movements,

even though (as we discussed in Chapter 11) most of us would be better off ignoring them, and

2) It's exceedingly difficult to avoid, even for those of us who know we should be doing our best to ignore it.

A Competition for Attention

A media company's revenue is a function of how much time and attention their viewers give them. The more viewers a TV show has, the more it can charge for its commercial slots. The more readers a newspaper has, the more it can charge for ad space. In short, media companies are all competing for your attention.

Financial media is no exception. Getting your attention—rather than giving you prudent financial advice—is priority #1. So it should be no surprise that—just like celebrity news, politics, and so on—financial news gets sensationalized to a remarkable degree.

"Experts" on TV

In addition to minute-to-minute market updates, financial news is filled with interviews of stock analysts, market analysts, and other financial

91

"experts." These interviews—which usually consist primarily of commentary on the day's stock market movements—tend to contain little of value.

But that shouldn't really surprise us, should it? After all, imagine what would happen if an expert came on TV and told the truth (i.e., that what happened in the market today is irrelevant for most investors, and that we'd be better off if we just stuck with a buy, hold, and rebalance strategy using low-cost index funds)? We'd stop watching after just one episode. Heck, most of us would stop watching after a couple of sentences—there's *got* to be something more exciting on TV, right?

Just Turn It Off.

The best way to deal with the problem? Turn off the financial news. Stop reading the financial section of the newspaper. Unfollow financial media sources on social media. And for those times that you *do* decide to give them your attention, remember: What matters to them isn't whether or not today's news is truly important. What matters is whether they can *convince* you that it's important. Do not be tempted to change your portfolio just because of something you saw on TV.

Chapter 15 Simple Summary

- Just like other media companies, financial news sources are engaged in a competition for your attention.

- We're bombarded with minute-to-minute stock market news, not because it's important, but because the media profits from us *thinking* that it's important.

- Resist the temptation to change your portfolio just because of something you saw in the news. The best way to do that is to stop watching financial news programs and stop reading financial news websites.

CHAPTER SIXTEEN

Steer Clear of Stock-Picking Newsletters

Stock-tip newsletters have been a constant presence in the investment industry for more than a century. Over the last couple of decades, they've only become bigger and more popular—with email obviously being far superior to printed newsletters for delivering timely information. And there are now countless Twitter accounts and blogs providing stock tips as well.

The danger in trusting a stock newsletter (or other similar publication), however, is three-fold:

1) Just like mutual funds, it's very difficult to know whether a newsletter's past performance is the result of anything other than

dumb luck,

2) Their advertised performance is not necessarily the performance they actually achieved, and

3) Even if the newsletter isn't fudging the numbers, it's unlikely that many of their subscribers actually achieved a similar level of performance.

Check the Fine Print

With mutual funds, at least, all the fund company can advertise is their *actual* performance. Next time you're online and you see a newsletter or "revolutionary trading strategy" being advertised, take the time to find and read the disclosure about how its performance was calculated.

Often, the performance calculations have been seriously convoluted in an attempt to make the advertised performance figure appear as high as possible. In fact, if you read carefully, you'll sometimes find that the advertised performance is purely hypothetical. (That is, the supposed hotshot investor didn't actually own any of the recommended stocks over the period in question. Rather, the performance advertised is for a strategy that was created based purely on hindsight.)

What Did the Subscribers Earn?

Even when the newsletter *is* advertising its legitimate performance, it's unlikely that many of the subscribers actually earned a return equal to that advertised. Why? Two reasons:

1) Advertised performance figures rarely include trading costs or capital gains taxes (both of which can be quite substantial for the rapid buying and selling strategies suggested by many newsletters), and
2) The newsletter's performance is typically calculated based on the assumption that the stocks in question were bought literally as soon as the newsletter was published. For most investors, that's simply not the case.

Given the dubious nature of the benefits provided by stock-picking newsletters, it's highly unlikely that they are worth your time, attention, or money.

Chapter 16 Simple Summary

- It can be tempting to follow the advice of an investment newsletter with an impressive performance record. But just like with mutual funds, it's almost impossible to be sure that a newsletter's performance is due to anything other than luck.

- The performance records advertised by many stock-picking newsletters can be rather misleading. Be sure to check how the figure was calculated.

- Due to trading costs and taxes, a newsletter's subscribers are unlikely to match the return of the newsletter itself.

CONCLUSION

Keep It Simple

It's no wonder that so many people find the topic of investing to be confusing. After all, we're constantly receiving conflicting messages about how to be successful investors.

For example, the mutual fund industry and the stock-tip-newsletter industry tell us that:

- Picking stocks successfully is difficult for the average investor, but
- A professional has a good chance of picking stocks that will outperform.
- A mutual fund (or stock newsletter) that has outperformed the market in the past is likely to outperform the market in the future.

At the same time, the discount brokerage firms are telling us that:

- Picking stocks on your own is easy!
- Rapid buying and selling of stocks (or other investments) is the best route to profits.
- With up-to-the-minute information, you can time the market successfully.

Meanwhile, the mainstream financial media is bombarding us with a third group of messages:

- Knowing what happened in the market yesterday (or last month) is essential for your success as an investor.
- If you watch the news enough and listen to enough economists/market analysts, you have a good chance of predicting the next market move.
- You can improve your performance by picking hot funds (particularly, those mentioned by a magazine).

So whom should we believe? *Each* of those sources seems like they should know what they're talking about.

The reality is that the primary goal of each of those parties is not to provide us with quality information, but rather to persuade us to consume their products (just like any other business). So we must tune them out and turn instead to unbiased sources of information (like academic studies).

When we do, we encounter a few findings that have been confirmed time and again:

- Within each category of mutual funds, expenses are the best predictor of future performance.
- Any investor—even a full-time professional—is unlikely to be able to reliably outperform the market.
- Reliably predicting short-term market moves is impossible.

And those facts lead us to a very simple investment strategy indeed: Diversify your portfolio using an asset allocation that's appropriate for your risk tolerance, minimize your costs using low-cost index funds or ETFs, and rebalance your portfolio whenever it strays far from your desired allocation.

APPENDIX

Helpful Online Resources

www.irs.gov
> The IRS's website. Has an abundance of easy to find information.

www.ObliviousInvestor.com
> The author's blog. Includes a wide variety of investing and tax-related articles.

www.Bogleheads.org/forum
> An online forum (named after the founder of Vanguard) with an active group of users with expertise on a range of personal finance topics.

About the Author:

Mike is the author of several personal finance books as well as the popular blog ObliviousInvestor.com. He is a Missouri licensed CPA. Mike's writing has been featured in many places, including *The Wall Street Journal*, *Money*, *Forbes*, *MarketWatch*, and *Morningstar*.

Also by Mike Piper:

Accounting Made Simple: Accounting Explained in 100 Pages or Less

Cost Accounting Made Simple: Cost Accounting Explained in 100 Pages or Less

Can I Retire? How to Manage Your Retirement Savings, Explained in 100 Pages or Less

Independent Contractor, Sole Proprietor, and LLC Taxes Explained in 100 Pages or Less

LLC vs. S-Corp vs. C-Corp Explained in 100 Pages or Less

Microeconomics Made Simple: Basic Microeconomic Principles Explained in 100 Pages or Less

Social Security Made Simple: Social Security Retirement Benefits Explained in 100 Pages or Less

Taxes Made Simple: Income Taxes Explained in 100 Pages or Less

Other Recommended Reading:

The Four Pillars of Investing, by William J. Bernstein

How a Second Grader Beats Wall Street, by Allan S. Roth

The Only Guide You'll Ever Need for the Right Financial Plan, by Larry E. Swedroe

The Power of Passive Investing, by Richard A. Ferri

A Random Walk Down Wall Street, by Burton G. Malkiel

Your Money and Your Brain, by Jason Zweig

INDEX

Made in the USA
San Bernardino, CA
08 January 2018